SPACESHIP

A COLLECTION OF WORDS FOR THE MISUNDERSTOOD.

OTHER BOOKS BY ROBERT M. DRAKE

SCIENCE

BEAUTIFUL CHAOS

BLACK BUTTERFLY

SPACESHIP

A Collection of Words for the Misunderstood.

Printed in the
United States of America
ISBN 978-0-9862627-4-6

Book design: Robert M. Drake

First Edition 2013

Dedicated

to all the lonely.

To the tired.

To the mutilated.

To the worried.

To the lost.

To the lovers.

To the hateful.

To the doubtful.

To the artist.

To the ordinary

and to the mad ones.

This book is

for

the misunderstood

The world is filled
with broken people
with broken lives
searching for broken love.
And that is why being
alone has never
felt so good.

I can't see myself
with the crowd.

I never have.

SPACESHIP

A Collection of Words for the Misunderstood.

People need people.

People need love.

They need to love themselves

the way they love

what they are sold.

CONTENTS

SPACESHIP

A COLLECTION OF WORDS FOR THE MISUNDERSTOOD.

THE SUN IS FALLING
AND I, TOO, AM FALLING
FOR YOU.
AND THERE IS NOT A
THING THAT COULD STOP ME
BECAUSE I DO NOT CARE.

SPACESHIP

A Collection of Words for the Misunderstood.

**she slept with wolves
without** fear**, for the
wolves** knew **a lion
was among** them**.**

drift, drift away and never return to the norm. And when you do come back, never, never drift towards the shores of the ordinary.

Look between the spaces, come lay

next to me. Now listen closely. I need you

to touch me like you own me. Dive into my

skin and force me to surrender. Make me forget

my name and only make me **remember** yours.

Lift me in the air so I can crash towards the

clouds and land in **your** arms. Now look between

the space inside my eyes and find the heal that

scorched this interest, so **passion**ately

towards you.

Sometimes, your side of the bed tells a certain

kind of story. Where your body would slumber

and leave these trenches within the bed sheets.

Well, sometimes I tend to **memorize** each crevice.

Sometimes, I even close **my** eyes and run my

fingers through each of them, so that the memory

of you would come lay and fill these **empty spaces.**

you float through **my world** leaving trails of color, over my skies.

What if a shy hello would spark a blaze. I stand firm, being. All while I wait for a glace of notice. Her voice like keys and my lust like the moon over her scape. To quench not, I thirst. Before my weary **eyes** stand alone, you for me and I, the classic fool to **believe in dreams**. I weep, for a lost love so deep; it crawls out of my bones.

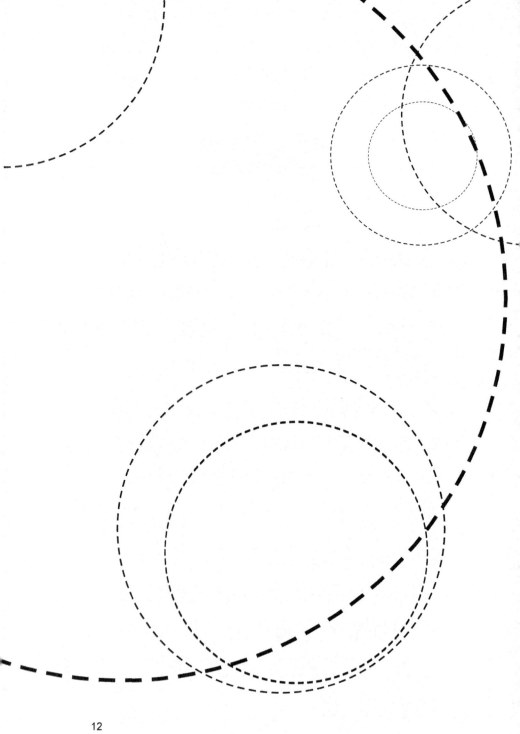

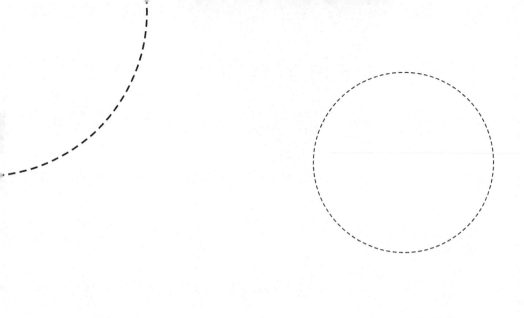

I **loved** **the**
way she spoke
while she stared
at the **stars**.

14

She stole my breath when **I** was willing to surrender

it. She had it all, everything the universe created

revolved around her gravity. Too much force! And

every day she drew my closer and closer. Until

forever faded away and there was nothing else but

the black of dead space. She stood with **her heart**

open and I, a shooting star that soared over her sky.

She understood me, I was half and without a

lingering sound, she knew I loved her. For my heart

spoke words I didn't want to say.

16

She was fierce, she was strong,

she wasn't simple. She was crazy

and sometimes she **barely** slept.

She always had something to say.

She had flaws and that was ok.

And when she **was down**, she

got right back up. She was a beast

in her own way, but one idea

described her best. **She was**

unstoppable and she took anything

she wanted with **a smile**.

18

We were doomed from the start
and what a tragic foreshadowing
it was. For we have all fallen in
love with life. And soon after, **death**
came in the room grinning,knowing
one day it would divorce us and
keep us separated forever.

Kiss like it's lost forever, love like the first time you looked into my eyes.

There she was, staring at the

television static with a blank face.

Her bruised lips stained a half lit

cigarette. Slightly tilted, she felt

pushed by waves of voices

convincing her she was perfect.

She knew she wasn't, she

was different inside! The wounds were

too deep. Her blood was violet

and suddenly violet became the

new black.

In the bloody stillness of the night, she stood in darkness. And colored the street with nothing, but a smile.

I wrote **her letters using my typewriter, she wrote me letters using** *her heart*.

This delicious **power** escaped from her stare. As if the room **wasn't enough**, so she lit my entire sky.

She defeated the **demons**
beneath her skin. But, she
could never rid the ones
buried within her bones.

Our beauty inspired God
to keep dreaming in color.

**Change
was
among**
*the
stars,* **the**
moment
**she
began to
love
herself.**

Somewhere along the way, she drifted into something I could never put into words.

We're **all wild flowers, waving underneath** the stars.

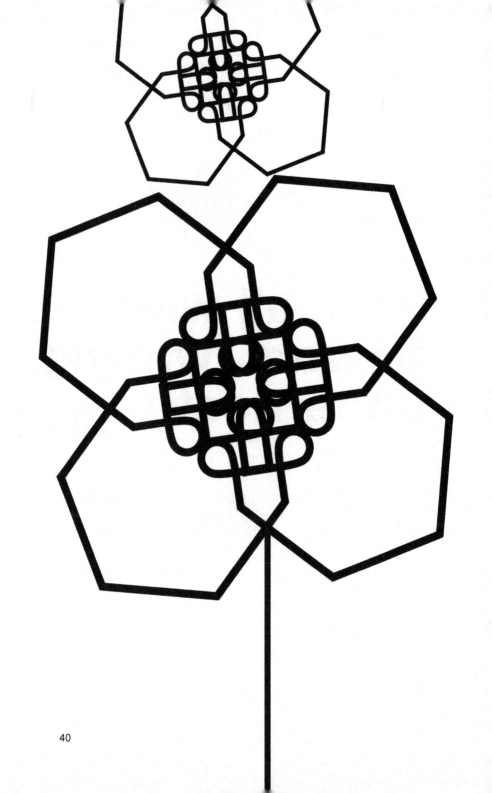

That night, *beauty did* not seek attention. And attention was *nothing*, without her beauty.

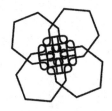

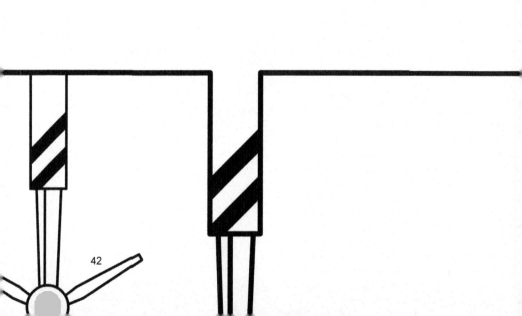

42

We're **all brain**washed.

My dear, every unread letter
I wrote you had a piece of
my soul. **A** collective **memory**
that reminded me how
special I could have been.

46

In the
chaotic
rubble,
she
still
remembered
who she
was.

48

She slugged her heart

towards these cracked

walls and *just like that*

it broke. That was the

beginning of *her adventure.*

Her heart *ran off* **and she**

had no choice but to

chase it.

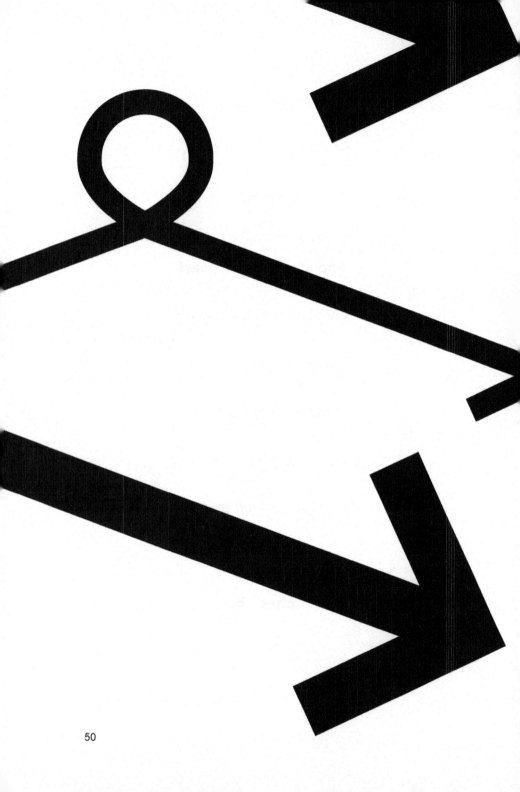

With eyes plucked so hate she saw not.

She just **wanted** to be happy. Her heart

squeezed like a sponge and flushed

memories adrift through heaps of wind.

So she blew away, across the flow and

forgot why the tears decorated **her smile**.

Destroyed by the friction the painful thoughts

would ignite. And in the chaotic rubble, she

still remembered who she was.

Dream with the dreamers and invent things

you never knew you had in you. Think with the

thinkers and discover ideas that mold who

you are. Smile at strangers **and** make friends

that last a life time. Laugh with friends and let

those memories burn through your heart. Travel

with travelers and **explore** a life beyond your

imagination. Love only one and grow old with

your best friend. Let these things bring fire to

your soul. So **when** you look back at your life,

you'll have no regrets. And **you can** leave this

place, better than when you found it.

54

To grasp the depths of love, we risk the monstrous grin of hatred.

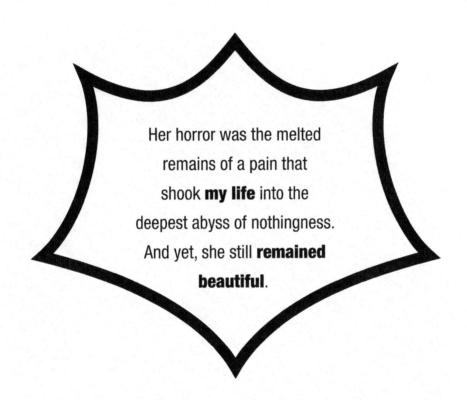

Her horror was the melted remains of a pain that shook **my life** into the deepest abyss of nothingness. And yet, she still remained **beautiful**.

I don't care if we don't have anything to say, *I just want* to be next to *you.*

She felt
interrupted
by everything
that moved
her.

The most precious moments
in life are usually **ignored.**

The wind whispered a destructive history **I wanted to** forget. But every time your name would **float**, my heart's waves would clash **violently** because I missed you.

She moved not, not one bit. **Stillness.**
Inside she burned alive. **Painless.**
Slowly opened her mouth and from the
darkness revealed her soul. **Stateless.**
Eyes pitched black. **Emptiness.**
With a cold deadly stare she spoke. **Nothingness.**
And the burst was not pretty, but the
monster the world turned her into. **Coldness.**

Listen.
Just you and me.
Follow, **follow**.
Right **this** way.
Let's burn together.
Into the **wild**.
Without **escape**.

The moon within

your eyes swallowed

my **sky** and the

very fabric of your

soul, **glowed** within

my heart.

And then God **slightly smiled, because we had no clue how closely drawn we were to one another.**

From this pain we grow scars to hide what s beneath our souls. And stay interrupted from a reality that lays within our naked bones.

She cared not of a broken heart. She cared of how she surrendered herself.

In the end, she had the courage to look faraway and let herself burn for the one she loved.

Imagine if I fell

apart, **melted**

all over your

body, profoundly

overpowered

you, as **you**

sweetly

surrendered

your

soul to

combine

with mine.

My scars remind me of where I've been, *your* **scars remind me of just how** *perfect* **you really are.**

I hugged you till **you** melted through

my arms. **Watched** you drip away onto

this pavement of nothingness. And the

ghost of your future passed with a

darkness so bright, it dissolved the

warmth in **my heart**, into the snowflakes

that comfort its coldness.

She wrapped herself in **attention** and **was** soaked with a suspicious **beauty,** too precious to be ignored.

We swept across *dreams like the rain.* Drowned both our demons and rested our heavy hearts in the black puddles we created.

An empty room
would still **be** a
beautiful place,
only if the
memory of you
crowds my heart.

Your eyes **always carried a certain kind of story, a mayhem of words.** *Misunderstood.* **And I was married to every sentence, because it devoured me from the start.**

Your eyes bloom; they're some

sort of window to your soul.

Because loving you isn't easy,

but everytime *you look* me in

the eyes, you grow far more

beautiful than the night before.

I have been **searching** my entire life.

Through every crack, under every rock,

I flipped the entire globe upside down

searching for something. Searching **for**

something, I've never seen. And in the

darkest hour, I just gave up. That's when

you found me.

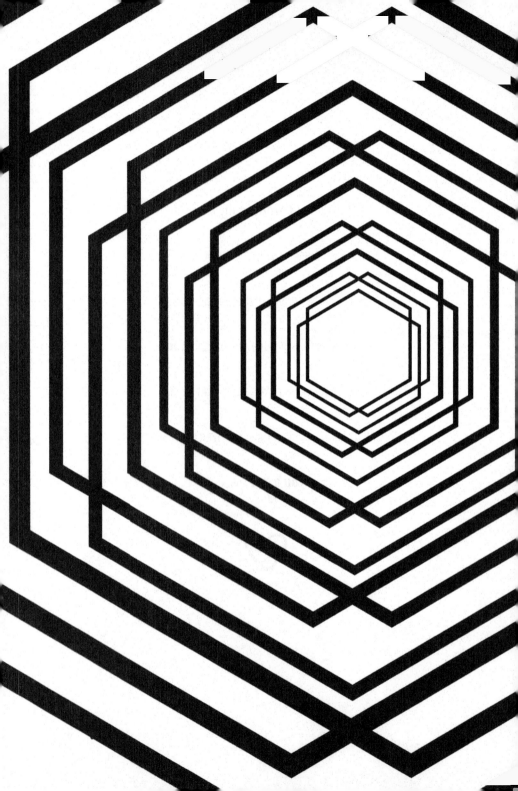

and the sky
smiled right
back at you, like
it knew a little more
about you,
each night.

Your gorgeous **chaos was a danger to my beautiful ordinary** life **and I knew that! Then suddenly, we became beautifully extraordinary together.**

If **loving**

you

kills me

tonight,

then

I was

ready

for

death

the

moment

you

said

hello.

We have all gone *beautifully* mad, in a *beautifully* mad world.

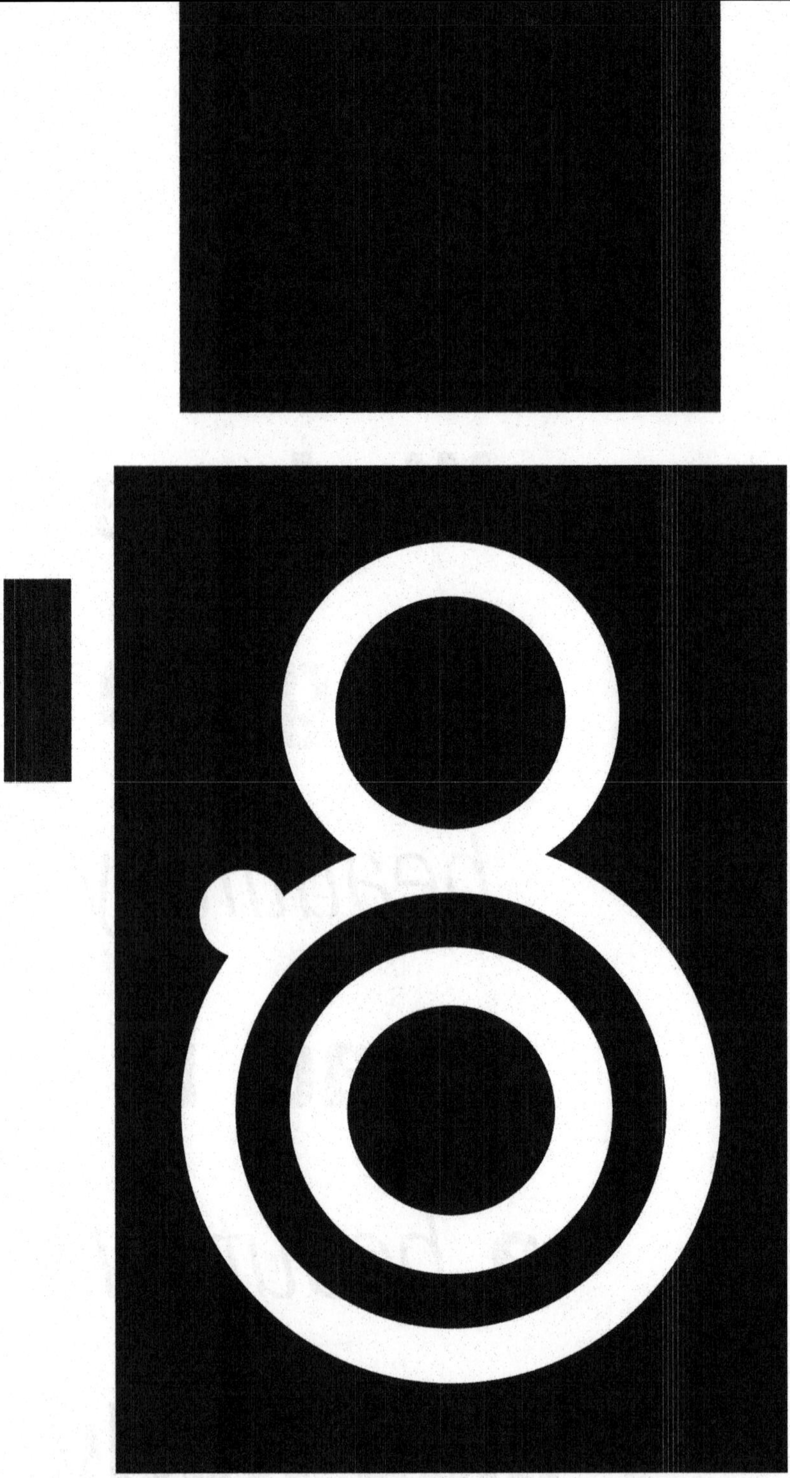

Remember the night you dissolved into the air and you told *me* to take a deep breath and inhale you in?

I've been holding my breath since.

Her eyes like a battered black sun, departed from the night before. She remembered **the suffering** the world **caused. But it was in her weary soul, a killer's instinct to savagely keep going.**

She painted beneath the break of tears and underneath **the** layers of pain, the sound of her **rain** carried a sweet tune worth loving.

Her faults

made her

interesting.

112

I knew her

once; **her**

deep faraway

eyes carried

a certain

shade

of pain.

And her

beauty

flourished,

the moment

I let her go.

She smiled at the ocean because the waves **told her story**.

And the stitches across *her* chest defined her past. So she presented her *heart* like some beautiful woman no man could ever resist.

118

We're all stumbling in the dark but we're far too close to the light to remain still.

Madness *is somewhere* **in**-*between chaos and having* **a dream**.

Let's love until it hurts and leaks.
So death sought after when we seek.

We love to death and love we speak.
Let's die for love, a love so deep.

Weep not, we slumber when we sleep.
It peaks within our bones and teeth.

What lies beneath it blurs in leaps.
Together in silence covered in sheets.

Let's die for love, a love so deep.
Forever love takes and plays for keeps.

LOVE IS A **TOUCH** *OF FRIENDSHIP AND A HANDFUL* **OF DREAMS.**

YOU COULD **NEVER** RECOGNIZE HAPPINESS, IF YOU HAVE NEVER **DANCE**D THE NIGHT AWAY **WITH SORROW**.

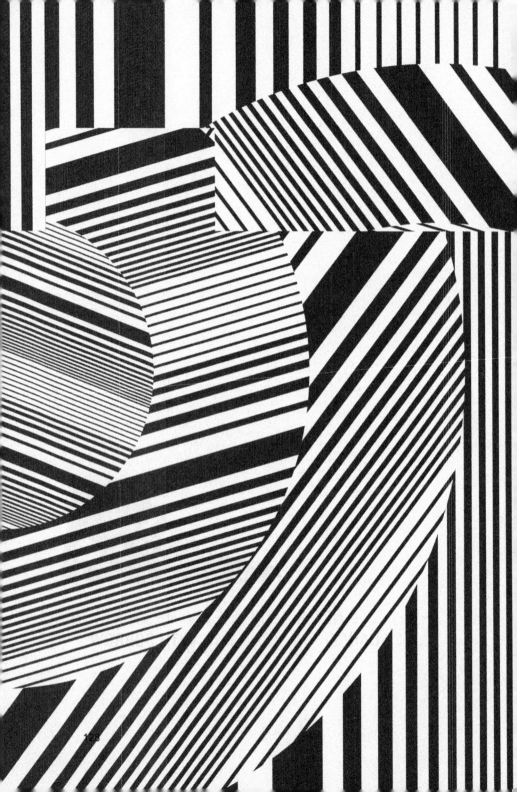

TO LET YOURSELF GO, IS TO *BURN WITH DESIRE* AND NEVER LOOK BACK.

I WANT TO LAY BENEATH WHATEVER COMES AFTER.
FEATHER WITHIN YOUR HEART AND HOWL DEEP ENOUGH
TO AWAKEN ALL THAT YOU ARE. POUR OUT MOONS AND
SKIES TO CREATE WORLDS FORGOTTEN BY THE STARS.
LAND SOFTLY IN YOUR ARMS, LAND SOFTLY IN YOUR
THOUGHTS. AND TOGETHER YOU AND I WILL HUNT
THIS LOVE AND CONQUER ITS RAIN UNTIL THERE'S
NOTHING LEFT BUT US. SOAKING BENEATH THE PUDDLE
OF DREAMS WE CREATED.

132

SOMETIMES, THE **GREAT**EST DREAMS
ARE THE ONES YOUR **HEART** FEARS.

SHE WAS A WILD FLOWER, A TIGER LILY WITH
A FEROCIOUS APPETITE. THERE WAS ALWAYS
A WAR IN HER HEART. I NEVER UNDERSTOOD
THAT. **LOST BETWEEN** CHASING **A DREAM** AND
STEPPING OVER STARS. AND SHE DESTROYED
EVERY BROKEN PIECE OF ME, IN THE MOST
BEAUTIFUL WAY. I WATCHED IT HAPPEN AND DID
NOTHING. BECAUSE BEFORE ME STOOD THE ONE
I LOVED AND I WAS WILLING TO BURN FOR
ANOTHER MOMENT TO WANDER IN HER EYES.

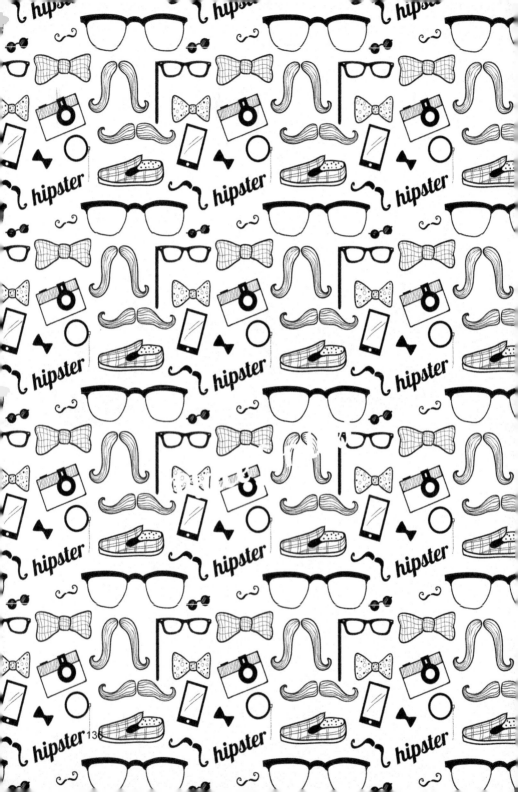

SOCIETY PUSHES US TO POUR OUT OUR BEAUTY AND UNIQUENESS. SO THEY CAN BURN US ALIVE FOR BEING TOO DIFFERENT.

OH SAD GIRL, IT'S OK TO CRY.
I TOO KNOW WHAT IT'S LIKE TO
BURY DEMONS ALIVE, KNOWING
ONE DAY THEY'LL *CRAWL OUT*.

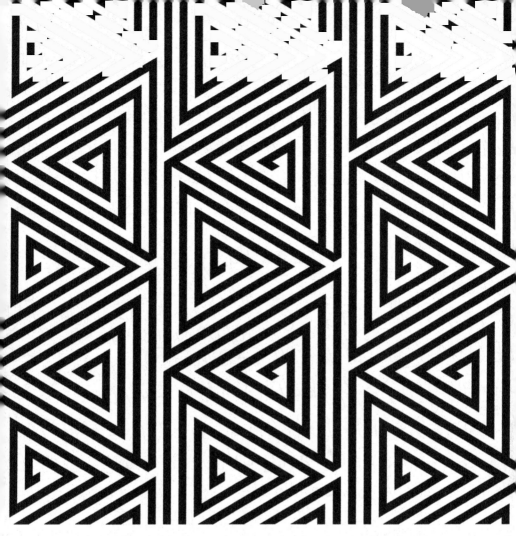

TRUST *IS* THE ONLY WEAPON IN THE CHAOS OF *LOVE*.

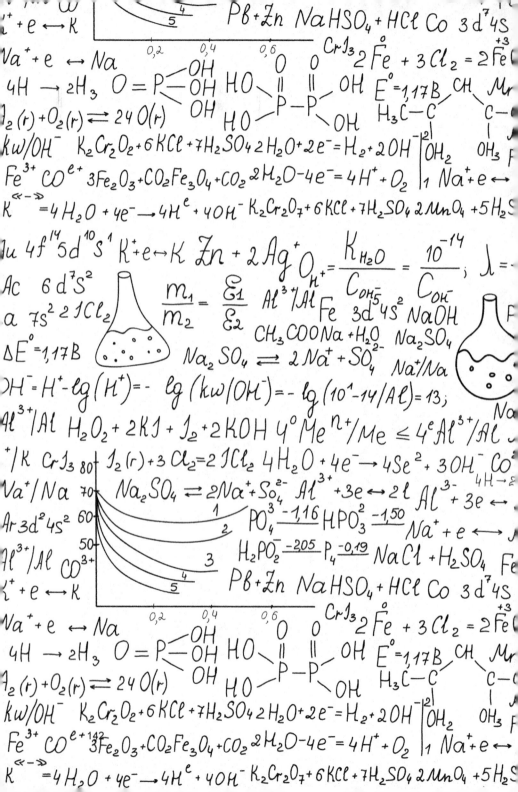

$$2Te + 3Cl_2 = 2TeCl$$

$$\underset{\overset{\|}{P}}{O} - \underset{\overset{\|}{P}}{O} \diagdown \begin{matrix} OH \\ OH \end{matrix}$$

$$E^0 = 1,17 B$$

$$H_3C - \underset{\underset{OH_2}{\overset{|}{|}}}{\overset{CH}{\overset{|}{C}}} \quad \underset{OH_3}{\overset{CH}{\overset{|}{C}}} - CH$$

$$Mn^2$$

$$Au$$

$$Pt$$

$$2H_2O + 2e^- = H_2 + 2OH^-$$

$$2H_2O - 4e^- = 4H^+ + O_2$$

$$1 \quad Na^+ + e \leftrightarrow N$$

$$_2Cr_2O_7 + 6KCl + 7H_2SO_4 \quad 2MnO_4 + 5H_2SO$$

**WHAT'S BENEATH
DEFINES US AND
MAYBE I'VE SEEN
TOO MUCH DARKNESS
TO IGNORE THE
DIMMEST SHINE
BURIED UNDERNEATH
THOSE LONELY
EYES.**

To Charise:

May your flame live
within me,
and continue to
inspire me
through every
waking hour.

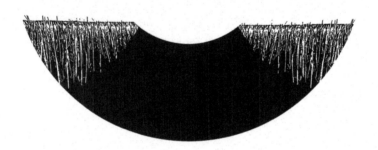

With open eyes I see the world,
with an open heart I see the souls
and with an open mind I see it all differently.

Thank you for your time.

Robert M. Drake

CHASING THE GLOOM

A NOVEL - FALL 2015

SUN FLOWER

ROBERT M. DRAKE

A NOVELLA
COMING SOON...

Also Available

ROBERT M. DRAKE

SPACESHIP

Also Available
ROBERT M. DRAKE
SCIENCE

ROBERT. M. DRAKE

beautiful
CHAOS

Follow R. M. Drake
for excerpts and updates.

Facebook.com/rmdrk
Twitter.com/rmdrk
Instagram.com/rmdrk
rmdrk.tumblr.com

CPSIA information can be obtained at www.ICGtesting.com
Printed in the USA
BVOW06s1932220416

445282BV00013B/71/P